IS YOUR BUSINESS HURTING YOUR SCHOOL?

21 LEADERSHIP LESSONS OF RUNNING A

BUSINESS CALLED "SCHOOL"

By

Stacey Owens Howard

Acknowledgments

Telling my story hasn't always been easy. Ten years ago, I would have never imagined the concept of writing a book; much less one opening my life in such a way for the entire world to see. I have been blessed with many angels during this journey called life and I would be remised not to acknowledge them.

Jacinta Clemon, thank you for the late-night conversations, the spiritual guidance and for being my Peter. You have given so much to my vision and dreams selflessly. It takes a special person to work 15-hour days to help someone else manifest their dream

My inner circle, Terrell Harris, Crystal Grey, Alexis Owens, Zechari Owens, Robert Owens, Sonja Owens, Carol Owens, Verta Henderson and Kevin Henderson; without you guys I would not be able to do what I do.

Table of Content

Introduction — Pg. 4

Chapter 1: School Economics — Pg. 7

Chapter 2: Marketing VS Recruiting — Pg. 19

Chapter 3: School as a Business — Pg. 24

Chapter 4: Managing the Business — Pg. 33

Chapter 5: Everyone Works for You — Pg. 50

Chapter 6: Communicating as a Business — Pg. 62

Chapter 7: Educational Systems — Pg. 67

Chapter 8: A Healthy Balanced Boss is Key — Pg. 72

Chapter 9: 21 Leadership: Lessons — Pg. 76

Chapter 10: The Charge — Pg. 100

Introduction

Have you ever needed to terminate an employee but just couldn't bring yourself to do so? If you answered yes, then you are not alone. I once felt that way and quickly realized my business ethics were hurting my business called "school".

Traditionally schools were designed to run as democratic infrastructures lead by mission statements with visions developed by various stakeholders. When the vision and mission work, it works, but what happens when it doesn't? What happens in low performing schools where the vision doesn't flourish? What happens when the environment is toxic and nonproductive? I will tell you what happens. Unfortunately the students fail and the school goes out of business.

In the industrial economy, production was based on the ability to perform large scale work in a single location using a factory concept. Schools were built on the backs of the industrial age movement. Using a one size fits all approach, schools prepared students to work in factories by teaching them how to read and write along with other basic topics such as math and history. Once employed, the company would provide on the job training that would prepare the student for the lifelong ability to work at the job. The economic goal was to complete school, work and retire.

Today's global demands require students to be able to work together, communicate and think creatively. The 21st century ushered in an economy based on informational technology. To be productive students must be able to be lifelong learners as the evolution of technology rapidly changes and improves every few years. In addition, schools must adapt and create new connections in order to ensure students are academically prepared and motivated to be productive.

The purpose of this book is to explore the business lessons learned as one leader dared to revolutionize the way school was done.

Chapter One: School Economic

In all schools the economy is generated by student enrollment. The number of students attending the school determines the amount of money the school receives for operation. So, as you may be able to see here, butts in seats are very important. Traditional schools have become very complacent with district lines providing a set number of enrollees. Principals in these settings spend little to no time marketing or searching for students as there is not necessarily a need to do so. This, however, is not the case for charter school or private school leaders. In the nontraditional educational setting parents make conscious choices to attend your school. Marketing and searching for new families is always at the forefront of almost every charter school leader. Any charter school leader who is not constantly thinking about obtaining and retaining student populations can be considered a failing charter school leader.

Coming from a traditional educational setting and being trained in a formal school setting gave me a false sense of security as a charter school leader. In my initial charter application, I was approved to open and operate with 450 students. My past educational experiences lead me to believe if I build it they will come. During my first few years in business I focused on all the wrong things. Such as making sure the staff wrote stellar educational plans, professional development plans and whatever other type of plans to ensure growth. Imagine my frustration as I began to ponder why it was so hard to increase by just thirty more students? I had the written plan right; yet, every year I came up short because I sat around waiting for my families to show up. This complacent behavior cost me to lose roughly $100,000 a year. Do that over a five-year timeframe as I did and watch a half of million dollars float out of your hands.

The business of school is to sell students the belief they can be successful, they can meet the requirements set by the state and then give them the tools in which to make that it happen. My charter school serviced students in grades k-8 so graduating students into the workforce wasn't the selling point for us. However, my staff is setting the stage as a feeder school for the local high school.

I had teachers who did not understand their role in selling students hope. These teachers would say things such as, "I don't have time to manage classroom data, Johnny is not going to pass the state exam he is just too far behind, or David get out of my classroom until you learn how to behave." These teachers totally misunderstood their role in the business of school. Classrooms equipped with this type of staff would experience high student turnover rates. School attrition was high and each year we would start with a new batch of students. I began to wonder, "What is the teacher's business role in school?"

I learned teachers must be great salespersons. The product in which they must be successful in selling is the future. This sell of the future includes getting students to meet deadlines, to believe in themselves, to learn to control their behaviors and do their job of learning so they can grow up and become law abiding, tax paying citizens.

What happens when your school business has poor salespersons? The customers, which in this case, are your parents, begin to take their business somewhere else. Unhappy parents will withdraw their student and move to another school they perceive will perform better. This causes lost in revenue and trust within the community as unhappy parents will often tell others.

I had a case where one of my teachers struggled with selling classroom behavior expectations to students. Everyday students were fighting and being disruptive. The teacher spent a great deal of time dealing with getting students to comply with her rules and expectations. The classroom disruptions caused a low rate of time on task. Good students lost trust in their teacher's ability to teach the class and began to complain to their parents. Parents would attempt to have conferences with the teacher and wouldn't be successful as the teacher never made time. I lost six students from that class totaling $24,000.

In the business world if an employee does not meet growth quota with his/her sales, the company will evaluate their level of production and set improvement goals. The very next month if production remains low, the employee would be terminated or moved to another department. In education, however, a nonproductive teacher can go throughout the entire school year not meeting goals. To make matters worse, the only drawback would be the teacher could receive an average written evaluation by the principal or be placed on an improvement plan. At the end of the year if the teacher continued to show little to no growth they would be handed a new batch of children to harm either at their current school or another within the district. It is a harsh and sad reality how teacher tenure makes it nearly impossible to remove a poor performing teacher out of the classroom.

The first four years in operation I followed the traditional school plan for improving teacher performance. Low performing teachers were placed on improvement plans, they received average teacher evaluations and at the end of the year they moved or returned to destroy another group of children. I provided professional development opportunities in support of their professional growth plans. This method, however, made no changes to getting the school off the low performance list and it just didn't make sense to me. I was pouring so much into the professional growth and development of my teachers yet my school was still failing. The school was listed as a continually low performing school, and our state report card grade was an "F". We lost an average of thirty kids each year which caused the school a financial loss of $144,000. In addition to the financial loss, each year marketing and finding new students also became an overwhelming struggle.

Entering the fifth year, I took a huge risk and invested the school's reserve fund of $59,000 into a renovation of a larger facility. To this point our student average daily membership (ADM) was around 116 students. With a larger space we could now accept up to 200 students. As a struggling school with a high attrition rate filling this new space would be a challenge. We managed to start our fifth year with 169 students. I was equipped with highly qualified teachers with five years or more experience and held master's degrees. I knew having the right people on the bus and in the right places was key for the success of the school. During the previous years a small budget had limited my ability to bring in experience. Upon entering my fifth year with a larger revenue, I took a risk and hired folks who looked great on paper, did well in their interviews and received excellent recommendations. I remember thinking,

"This year shall be great," only to be disappointed within the first 60 days of operation. It was at this time I decided to change my way of doing school and follow the business aspect of sales and production. I came up with a plan which included posting everyone's job, setting a standard for daily production, and then evaluating everyone on their ability to produce results. In a ten-month period, following this business mindset, I terminated nine non-productive teachers. These positions were then quickly filled with motivated staff members who understood the role of strong parent communication, monitoring student behavior, and effective daily planning for teaching and learning. Students began to do their job, resulting in positive scores on our end of year state testing. This decision not only saved the school $40,000, we also made a major accomplishment by meeting our student growth goals.

America is built on economics. In the industrial age, schools started to assume the important role of producing skilled labors who could aid in the development of a better economy. An economic problem occurs when students drop out of school. The chances of them spending time unemployed or receiving government assistance increases dramatically in areas where dropout rates are high; local, state and federal government feel the impact as these individuals are not capable of paying taxes. In addition to lower tax revenue, local and state governments with less educated populations face greater challenges with attracting new business investments and pay more on social programs. Therefore, the goal of the school is to produce tax paying citizens who are able to gain employment and entrepreneurship.

A school productive in selling the idea of hope, can show students how to build on their talents and empower them to believe in their future is a school impacting the economy.

Chapter 2: Marketing vs. Recruitment

If students are the main source for building revenue how do you find them? I spent a lot of time thinking about and discussing marketing for students in the early years of operation. During the first three years, money was tight; therefore, it was difficult setting some aside for marketing purposes. Nevertheless, I developed a marketing plan consisting of placing articles and ads in the local newspaper, and even created flyers, brochures, magnets, post cards and signs. Despite my best efforts no one saw this stuff. As it turned out within the population I served, parents did not read the newspaper. Another obstacle was the fact that many apartment complexes and businesses did not allow flyers to be posted as it was considered a form of solicitation. It was a challenge to say the least getting volunteers and staff to efficiently pass out or post flyers throughout the community.

After several failed attempted to gain students from the strategies listed in our marketing plan, the team met and decided to revise the plan to now include digital marketing techniques. A website and Facebook page was created along with previous marketing items. We also thought it was a great idea to post pictures and other items to give the community insight into all the wonderful things we did as a school. And yet, despite our efforts, still we struggled to grow the student population by a simple thirty students.

In a desperate move to figure out why the billboards, Facebook page, website, newspaper articles, flyers and brochures were falling on deaf ears; we decided to survey everyone who walked through the door by asking, "How did you hear about us?" To my surprise parent referrals was the number one response followed by online. As it turns out, happy parents were telling others. The only question to ask ourselves now was how do you build on this?

I spent five years sitting on my behind, putting paper out in the environment hoping others would stumble across them, read it and coming running. At the end of my fifth year it was apparent if I was going to fill the 200 slots and have a waiting list, I needed to learn the difference between marketing and recruiting.

The marketing tools created and used in the early years played a huge part in the branding efforts. They told what we were doing and conveyed information to parents and community members. Now I needed to communicate the same message in a different way in order to recruit a high-quality staff. Improving the staff as part of the recruitment process increased the number of happy parents, which in turn, increased our referrals.

Current parents were responsible for a large percentage of new student enrollment because of referrals. To capitalize on that we provided several parents with great talking points aligned to our brand. We also asked new families to share who referred them and the referring parents were eligible to win gift cards.

A street team was soon implemented to make home visits to the families who completed the lottery application. This team personally had delivered a welcome package inclusive of the acceptance letter and other items to the new families. This face to face personal interaction created a positive response from the new families. To our surprise, they told their friends and then they applied within days. This intentional effort of getting out of the office and actively recruit parents turned out to be the most effective method. Recruitment must be a yearlong process and should always include actively sharing the great things going on within the school.

Chapter 3: School as a Business

Graduating Summa Cum Lauda from a School of Administration Master's program prepared me for leading a school. However, it did not prepare me for running the business of school. I learned about budgets, grants, revenue sources from state entities and that education is the responsibility of the state based on the state's constitution. At the University level administrators are trained to manage the basic needs of all stakeholders.

In 2013, I had the distinct pleasure to open a charter school. In the early years I used - my formal training from the Master's program to design and run the school, and I failed miserably. The first four years were riddled with lots of errors that made no cognitive sense because I followed the textbook model to a T. Armed with my knowledge of budgets and taxation for education; I was given $500,000 of state and local funds to operate my school without any capital funding to assist with securing a facility. I quickly learned banks would not fund charter schools because of their non-profit business structure. I learned board of directors and charter school leaders needed to have assets to cover any loans. I learned - state funding could only be used for leasing and not purchasing; so the school had no assets to cover loan requests. I also learned bonds voted on by local governments did not apply to charter schools, yet many would say school is not a business.

For four years I held school in a 3,000 sq. ft. building that was once the organizations afterschool facility. The school was approved to operate with 400 students but only 98 students could fit in the afterschool site. I then learned that any school with less than 200 students was on a path for financial suicide. I ended the school year in the red and placed on financial probation with the state department.

Entering the following school year in the red placed the school on financial noncompliance with the Department of Public Instruction. The budget is set on a projected number based on student enrollment. Employment contracts are issues prior to the start of school based on the same projections. Limited energy was given to marketing and searching for new families. I thought I could not afford to put together a huge marketing campaign due to my financial limitations. This was a huge rookie mistake for it takes money to make money. Having the mindset of holding on to money and not spending did not correct my financial issues; in fact this made matters worse. We started the year 50 students less than our projections which created a $300,000 loss of projected revenue. To correct the shortage I cut several programs and operated on bare bone resources. At the end of the day, that still wasn't enough to balance the budget. With the threat of losing my state charter if financial issues were not corrected, lead to me imposing a 15% budget cut across the board in the middle of the year. Can you imagine telling your contracted teachers you must cut their salary by 15%? They were not happy and some decided to leave. Cutting salaries mid-year of contracted personnel wasn't a common practice in the traditional setting. Teachers were not use to being promised a set pay for the year and then faced with losing pay. This was one of the toughest decision I had ever made, but without the budget cuts I was tracked to end the year $80,000 in the red.

From a funding perspective, private school's parents pay the school directly for services. If parents are unhappy with the school's performance, they can make the decision to remove the child. Public schools are funded by tax money provided by the government. Parents are indirectly paying the school and have less recourse of action to take if they are unsatisfied with the school's performance. Charter schools have the unique ability to fit between both the private and public sectors of schools. Funding is provided by state, local and federal government through taxation. However, if a parent is not happy with the level of production they can withdraw their children and create the same effects that are created in the private school. Charter schools must operate as a business as it is dependent on its customers (parents) and responsible for maintaining and gaining its own private infrastructures.

We were the only charter school in the area and offered several program options that were not available in the district. For example, we offered an extended day program which kept children in school for ten hours. The 8am to 5pm school day was ideal for working parents who could not afford childcare. We also offered art integration using a performance arts model. Students were able to use the creative side of their brain which helped with those who struggled with the traditional "sit and get" methods of teaching and learning. My parents loved the new school concept as they were unhappy with the experience from the traditional school. Parents wanted the extended day program that allowed students to be in school for ten hours, but they would not participate in fundraisers to aid in obtaining funding to support the school. We had two out of service buses that traveled across the county requiring students to be on the bus or in school for 14-hour days. Ninety percent of the parents had means of transportation but did not want to carpool or bring their child to school because they didn't want to use their gas. Parents wanted a larger facility but could not conceptualize how they could aid in assisting with obtaining one. Many of my families operated from a rather poverty stricken mindset, therefore, they were not equipped with bringing support to the school.

What other means of funding could we generate as a school? What marketing improvements were needed to reach the base of the families we served? What steps do we take to find and retain our student base?

Entering my fifth year I concluded school is a business and if I didn't start treating it as such I would be out of business and back to working for someone. I surrendered and sought outside help. It was during this intervention I learned the business of school was hurting my school. Principals and superintendents often enter the field as trained teachers with little to no training in management, labor relations, systems, communication and logistics. It is often these areas that suffer most in low performing schools.

Chapter 4: Managing the Business

Employees are the main vessel of any business. Having the right employees can create a productive and thriving organization. Schools must become good at identifying, developing and retaining good teachers.

What determines or define the characteristics of a good teacher/employee? I once thought credentials and experience defined high quality teachers. Armed with 12 teachers who had master's degrees, a state teaching license and five or more years of experience; I was ready to have the best school year yet. Unfortunately, it didn't go as well as planned. All 12 of my highly qualified teachers struggled with reaching and teaching the broken students that were in their classrooms. The criteria I used to identify highly qualified teachers consisted of finding those who had completed the academic processes of becoming a professional teacher. I did an excellent job at identifying those who completed the process of becoming a teacher. What this method failed to identify was unhealthy mental state, the lack of passion and compassion towards others, or the personal trauma rooted in their past that defined the adult they had become.

Donna obtained her Master's degree in psychology to compliment her Bachelor's degree in Education. It was her desire to enhance her general education classroom with peer mentor sessions that would help at-risk children learn how to maneuver through uncomfortable social settings. Donna herself had experienced a very traumatic life event and felt therapy had been very beneficial for her and it was only right for her to give that same feeling to others. Donna's false sense of healing created a person who failed to focus on educating the students in her classroom. Her strong desire to save children from experiencing life as she once had was the fuel to her designing a therapeutic classroom environment. Donna spent more time counseling her students through group play, peer mentoring and individual counseling than teaching core subjects. These discussions brought out false or over aggregated feelings from students. Students began to complain about her digging into their personal life without reason. Trust issues were formed, and students wanted to be removed from the classroom. Academic growth within the classroom was not occurring. Quarterly benchmark assessments showed a digression in student performance.

Donna struggled with preparing the curriculum components of the classroom. In addition to that, she also felt the professional duties of teaching such as maintaining report card grades, conferencing with parents and lesson planning was expecting too much from teachers and required too much personal time. Time management was a major concern for Donna. She did not feel teachers should have to complete any duties at home or on the weekends.

Our students attend school from 8am to 5 pm, having students and staff on campus for a nine-hour day. By design I ensured teachers had a 90-minute planning block four days per week. Administration didn't plan trainings or meeting during this time to allow time for teachers to plan effectively and complete the required professional duties. Unfortunately, this time was often not used for its intended purposes by most teachers with the end result being teacher burnout. Donna's views on professional duties of teaching hindered her from meeting deadlines and maintaining accurate records for student progress. Needless to say, her refusal to complete professional tasks eventually lead to termination. This was a great teacher on paper in terms of her credentials but in practice she was functionally depressed and not productive in the classroom. The most surprising part of this termination was the reaction received from students and parents. Both groups contacted me afterwards and stated they wish I had done it much sooner.

When identifying great teachers it is imperative to look more so at the content of their character. Find individuals who are engaging, dedicated and passionate about teaching and willing to be open to learning. The level of education, ability to meet the eligibility guidelines of state licensure and experience are excellent criteria to use, but should not stand alone in the identification process.

Teacher development is another important role of managing the business. With the ever-changing processes used to develop students, teachers must be able to evolve and grow in the profession. Training programs and professional development are the main sources used for teacher development. What happens when teachers are not influenced by the training program?

Karla, equipped with a Master's degree and several years of teaching experience, struggled with accepting personal growth. To her, attending training and receiving constructive feedback was considered the administration's way of trying to change her educational beliefs and practices. Karla strongly felt there was no need for change and simply wished to be left alone. Her strong personality attracted insecure co-workers to follow her and seek advice for their personal growth. In many incidents, feedback provided by the administration and Karla often contradicted each other. This caused confusion and stopped the growth of several staff members. Before one realized what was happening, a toxic environment was birthed, and it was the students who began to suffer.

  During our annual staff retreat, teachers were instructed to focus on lesson planning and teaching strategies. They were also required to plan a twenty-minute lesson to teach at the retreat. Coworkers completed peer observations and provided anonymous written feedback while administration provided verbal feedback. Having to teach in front of peers turned out to be very insightful. Teachers who were perceived as great showed themselves as needing improvement, while several new or less experienced teachers who lacked confidence, knocked the assignment out the box. Their natural passion for teaching showed as well as the hard work they put into preparing for the assignment. This instructional highlight was a turning point for personal and professional growth for every single teacher. Karla was able to observe what excellent teaching looked like and was personally challenged in her own self reflections. It was that day Karla lost her following and the insecure teachers' observations of different colleagues lead them to connect with others. Social structures and click groups among the teaching staff were crushed and everyone began to take responsibility for the own personal growth. "You can't grow if you don't know" was the main takeaway from the retreat.

A training program that provides a model of expectations, opportunities for teachers to practice the model, and follow up with administrative feedback; ensures professional growth in teacher development. Everyone must be held accountable for getting better.

Managing the business also comes with a need to carry a certain level of confidence allowing one to walk in authority. As the leader of a charter school you are the principal, superintendent and the overall boss of the organization. As an African American female director, I faced employee disrespect on a regular basis. Initially, I did not know how to recognize employee disrespect.

One example of employee disrespect occurred while I was out sick for a few days. I spent the entire summer building up the confidence of the staff and setting the direction for the course of the year. A minor surgery required me to be hospitalized for a week. One employee spent that entire week undoing all that had been done during the summer. She built alliances and convinced coworkers to follow her beliefs. This coworker had a unique ability to build up the confidence of employees suffering with low self-esteem. They believed everything she told them and blindly aimed to please her. Interestingly, behind their backs she laughed at them, talked about their inability to manage the classroom and even told me every one of them will quit due to their inability to perform. This employee disrespected the school's culture and administrative process by dealing with issues and assuming roles that were not hers to assume. When confronted she became very hostile and used nonverbal body language movements, symbolic for fighting in the streets. There was no recovery from this type of behavior and termination was inevitable.

Never ever allow anyone to disrespect you as a leader or the business. It is a privilege to be part of a journey that is saving the lives of young people and those who make the choice to join the journey must know and understand their worth and contribution to the cause.

"Having the right people on the bus in the right seats," is a common cliché' used to express the importance of surrounding yourself with the right people. As the leader of an arts school, I like to say, "Having the right people standing at the canvas holding the right brush is important." My brief study of failing charter schools, in particularly those lead by African American owners, showed a common thread of hiring practices amongst family or friends who were not qualified to do the assigned job.

One example of this included a charter school located in an adjacent county. The school experienced financial and academic hardships which eventually lead to the school closing. It later came out in the news that the charter school leader was a financial advisor who had no previous experience or formal training in governing a school. The second person in charge was a family member who also did not have any formal training.

When operating in a leadership position with the authority of hiring family and friends will come expecting an opportunity to work within the organization. I am not against hiring family or friends, but I do feel all hiring must be to benefit the business. Having a strong nepotism policy in place to govern how family members will be supervised while employed is key. Most importantly, positions should be filled with those who are qualified to do the job and be productive.

Writing and implementing policies are also a huge part of managing the business of school. These policies govern the conditions required to ensure students and staff work together effectively. Interestingly, the nine terminations which occurred during year five were all based on personal conflict with business practices; not one was based on teacher classroom performance. Let's discuss policy.

While driving to work an employee experiences a minor traffic conflict that turns into road rage. The employee continues driving to campus fully aware that the person of conflict is following them. Upon reaching campus the employee hops out the car, enters campus and clocks into work. After clocking in, the employee returns to the parking lot to continue arguing with the angry driver who is showing a gun on his hip holster. This argument occurs in front of other staff and their children without any notification given to administration or local police. The employee was terminated for fighting on school grounds. I also had to review the policy on clocking in and work behaviors.

In another scenario, the teachers' workday began at 7:30 am and students' day began at 7:50 am; allowing staff twenty minutes to prepare for the workday. However, 95% of the staff reported to work five to fifteen minutes late regularly. Many would walk into the building with the students and classroom observations showed ill prepared teachers struggling with classroom management and student behaviors. It didn't take long for me to implement a late policy. The policy stated if a staff member incurred a third unexcused tardy, it resulted in a deduction of a half day's pay. Losing a half day's pay quickly changed the culture of reporting to work late.

Spending time reflecting on how you want to manage your business and staff is imperative. Once you determine the way to run the school, take time to create written policies clearly communicating daily operating procedures. I had major policies dealing with harassment and how to handle grievances, however, at the end of the day it was the smaller things lacking policy which started to beat the business.

Chapter 5: Everyone Works for You!

Open your mouth and scream out loud, "Everyone works for me!" While this may seem like a simple understanding occurring with automaticity upon gaining employment; unfortunately, some employees miss this connection after accepting the job. I encountered several strange employee relationships within the early stages of starting the school to say the least.

It appeared I struggled with understanding the law of attraction. This may be due to the fact that I came from a place of brokenness. I figured out very early in life if I wanted things to be different I had to learn how to turn my lemons into lemonade. Becoming an entrepreneur and independent business owner was not in my playbook of life. I didn't have a master plan, formal business training or any other guides to becoming a boss. All I had was a dream, motivation and the determination to be successful. I figured if I was obedient to following the dream the rest would follow. I can only imagine the frequent thoughts of overcoming lurking in my unconscious mind.

The constant thought of making a drastic change in my life became a beacon of light for other broken people wishing for the same. You might be asking, "What's wrong with that?" The problem with attracting likeminded people was actually my incompletion in my personal healing. It was easy for people to see my outer shell, progress and success. What they didn't see, however, was the personal changes, sacrifices, fear, hard work, dedication and the often heavy toll put on those closest to me.

Just imagine attracting several broken people filled with hope; of course they don't reveal this at the interview. Hidden agendas are soon formed and now you have employees who are battling internally and you as the boss have no idea what you are dealing with. The interview would good well, the job would be offered and then the other side of the employee would emerge.

My initial desires were to help those who are in need. As a boss, I would have people who were not acting or working in the best interest of the company. I did not like creating situations that would cause someone to become unemployed. I would over compensate and pour a lot into helping individuals who didn't realize they needed to help themselves. This created a culture of entitlement; employees who felt it was my responsibility to make things easy for them and to conform to their needs. These same employees did not feel it was their job to be productive or accept the ultimate responsibility of changing the lives of children.

      They became manipulators, victims or revengeful. I found myself trying to avoid conflict or making folks angry by allowing behaviors and actions to manifest that would have never been allowed at any other school or business. The funny thing was the same people I covered, poured into or looked out for were the very ones who would be disloyal and leave me in a bind when they determined it was no longer a good fit for them. These were the ones who would be the least productive in the organization and the root of toxic behaviors.

I walked through the first four years as an entrepreneur with an employee mindset. I got up, went to work and acted just as a regular employee would. Imagine that, here I am the CEO/founder of a nonprofit and charter school behaving as though I was an employee of the organization. I wrote the nonprofit bylaws, the 501 (3) c, the grants for funding and the charter for the school all by myself with the help of self-help books, yet, I still thought of myself as an employee. I signed my own paycheck for seven years and still did not know what it meant to be a boss.

Thankfully, I was smart enough to know when to reach out for help and brought in an outside consultant.

Having an employee mindset will create an atmosphere for others to come into your space and tell you what to do. Working with my first consultant started out great. As any good employee I placed myself in a position to learn and follow directions. For two years this consultant provided coaching sessions, made site visits and provided training to help my low performing school. Some changes and improvements were made but some poor behaviors intensified and continued to manifest. The initial request for help was to assist with leadership development and getting the school into compliance.

Slowly, the consultant began to move into other areas such as curriculum and building school culture. With my employee mindset I allowed these gradual changes without asking questions or providing direction. However, after reflecting on areas that were not progressing, I thought it would be a good idea to bring in another consultant specializing in behavior development. I did not see this as a conflict as both consultants specialized in different areas. I figured if we all worked together things would move faster.

The relationship with my first consultant began to change. We communicated less due to manipulation and fear. I was well aware of my daily struggles so having a consultant pointing out the school deficiencies by accusing the administrative leaders of not being effective communicators was not productive. Every meeting somehow always lead to a discussion of how the staff was not listening to administration and it was because the leaders did not know how to lead. Trust issues were developing and I began to build a wall of protection around my thoughts and feelings.

The consultant then began to suggest major changes that would take the school in a direction not aligned to the school's vision. The most hurtful thing I experienced in the process was hearing the person who I hired to help bring about change say, "You will not meet your goals and the school will continue to be low performing." Once again, I found myself in a weird, conflicting relationship. Here it was I had hired a consultant for help, yet, he was not listening to my thoughts and using fear tactics to influence my decisions.

One of the first things I was asked by Dr. Jackson was, "Stacey you do realize everyone works for you right?" To be honest, up until that very moment, I had never looked at it like that. I was just showing up to work like a good employee. He began the journey of showing me how my employee mindset was killing my boss moves and if I didn't learn the difference I was doomed to become a full-time employee working for someone else. As I began to learn what boss moves looked like, sounded like and felt like; the rose-colored lens began to fall off my eyes. I began to learn how my behaviors were creating entitled employees who were disrespectful. I learned how my employee behaviors of allowing everyone to operate on my same level was causing confusing lines of communication and conflicting relationships. When I speak of levels, I am certainly not saying I was better than anyone but there are different levels between boss/leader and employees.

Dr. Jackson would always emphasize, "Stacey everyone works for you; even me." At the end of the day I could take his advice or leave it, because as the boss, I was the only one who had to deal with the consequences. I learned to communicate my expectations and needs for the company without the fear of what others thought about my choices. I stop falling to the back during those critical discussions and stepped into my role as boss. Although I lost many along the way; I learned to activate my voice of authority. I learned two value lessons from the relationship with my first consultant: (1) Business relationships are not friendships. (2) People hired to help are not your partners.

I had a good relationship with my first consultant, and although it was easy for us to talk with each other, at the end of the day I still hired him. He was my employee; not my friend. Once those lines became blurry and I began to exhibit boss qualities he became threaten and abandoned the mission. An attempt was made to convince me having multiple people to counsel me was the problem, but I knew it wasn't. Be careful of what you listen to and allow to become your truths.

I also made the mistake of treating my consultants as business partners. It was easy to think of them this way as I worked with them because they knew all of the intimate details after all. Understand this; a partner is someone who puts the same amount of money, effort, blood, sweat and tears into the project. My consultants were getting paid to deliver a service. They were not with me during the time I was seeking funds, writing grants and carrying the weight of the organization; therefore, they were not my partners.

Chapter 6: Communicating as a Business

Communication as a leader requires one to be direct, specific and clear. Leaders spend a great deal of time communicating with staff, students and parents. It is the one single act sure to take place all day, every day. As the boss it is important to know yourself. You must be aware of your communication style, use of body language and other nonverbal communications to your employees. Messages can easily become lost in interpretation if communication skills are not planned and well thought out.

Communication comes in many forms, verbal, nonverbal, written and virtual. Verbal communication begins with clarity. To ensure clarity it simply requires one to slow down and speak thoughtfully. Often when communicating verbally people are quick to answer questions or to add to the conversation. By taking time to think before responding and not interrupting the flow of the conversation, a more thoughtful and clear conversation can be held.

Nonverbal communication is a can be considered as a continuous form of communication; it is always going on. Your body language is constantly speaking, and others notice it even when you are not aware of what your body is saying. Body language tells how you feel and expresses your true thoughts through eye contact, posture, voice tones, gestures and even how you position yourself among your colleagues. Those who can communicate effectively non-verbally can reinforce what they are saying verbally with confidence.

Verbal and nonverbal communication is important and requires the help of effective listening. Effective listening improves interpretation and accurate responses. Listening completes the communication loop.

Effective communication requires one to be confident in knowing the knowledge that will be communicated. As the boss all communication is designed to directly or indirectly impact the desired student outcomes.

As the boss of a low performing school it often felt as though several of the low performing teachers were not listening. Although I provided a lot of professional development; I saw little change within their personal development. I often wonder how someone could have coaching sessions, professional development training and detailed evaluative feedback, yet still not grow, change or increase personal production.

    I was well in tune to the mission and academic goals designed to remove the school off the low performing list, however, I wasn't in tune to my lack of social awareness of others. I was not in tune to the fact that 100% of my staff was emotionally starved. The low performing teachers were struggling professionally and wanted help but naturally were cautious with revealing the need. It appeared they also were not connected to the root of their emotional deficiencies. My cognitive brain was driving the way I communicated with my staff. I followed the school's leadership blueprint to a T but yielded no positive results. It wasn't until my social awareness kicked in and showed me I needed to tap into my other interpersonal skills. My emotional intelligence had to be natured and groomed. I had to learn how to tap into the emotional IQ of each of my staff members. Being aware of emotions and managing them can lead to greater focus where goals may then be achieved. I had to take responsibility for creating a positive environment and providing opportunities for everyone to improve. Staff members had to take responsibility for personal growth and change. This concept was clearly communicated.

Chapter 7: Educational Systems

Art integration is the foundation of our instructional program. When looking at the management of our teaching and learning systems, a lot of energy was put into the elements of art integration only to produce the need for extensive professional development with little impact on student progress. With no formal training in system thinking, I struggled as a leader to harmoniously facilitate all the systems to produce the desired level of student success.

I spent time reviewing all systems within the school to ensure they were working as separate systems. I failed at managing the school using a system thinking as the catalyst for change. Hindsight being 20/20, I have learned to improve teacher quality by ensuring teachers improve their personal selves. Spending $15,000 on professional development, training the teachers to use software and other curriculum products, had less of a return on my investment. I had a greater return on the money I spent bringing in a licensed counselor who skillfully showed teachers a map of themselves and challenged them to deal with their personal shortfalls.

Being a small school with a limited budget, I often operated under a poverty mentality. I would spend money on tons of paper to copy worksheets but would not spend money on items that would change the course of a student's life. However, in my fifth year, I increased spending in resources that invested into the students and aided in increasing their knowledge of what was required to become successful adults. I also decided to go out on a limb and tell the students I would take all students who met their end of year growth goals to an amusement park. I conferenced with each student personally and asked if they had ever been to an amusement park. To my surprise 98% of the student body had never experienced an amusement park nor did they have any idea as to what it was. To say they were very excited for the opportunity to go is an understatement. Students began asking their parents to get them tutors so they could meet their goals. Class participation increased and students who were previously unmotivated suddenly became motivated. My only wish is that I would have imposed the idea sooner than two weeks before testing.

This one trip on a chartered bus changed the lives of so many students. It was the incentive that gave them a purpose to complete a task.

Systems are a set of elements which function to accomplish a common purpose. In schools, systems consist of teaching, learning, funding and resource allocation to human resources and staffing. Educational systems are complex, which often makes reform efforts challenging.

Systems are characterized by synergy and are dependent upon an exchange of energy that bonds all elements of the system together into a healthy functioning relationship. One issue with educational systems is that they are regarded as open systems. The open systems operate in isolation of each other. My experiences showed me in the school business opens systems must be closed.

Chapter 8: A Healthy Balanced Boss is Key!

Running a business requires time, energy, and personal sacrifice. When taking on the role of entrepreneur one must be able to balance both their professional and personal selves. In the early stages I did not work to ensure I ruled from a healthy state. I carried the burden of the school alone and worked day and night to survive the foundational building years. Knowing the first five years would be challenging, and if not managed correctly could fail, I put everything except the business on the back burner. This did not prove to be the best method. My personal life was soon under attack. January of year two of the business, my daughter informed me she was expecting a child. Not being able to fully care for herself and unmarried, she needed my emotional support to help her determine the next steps she should take in her life. I didn't connect and continued to work harder at the business.

Four months later my son was diagnosed with stage four Large B Cell Lymphoma surrounded by T-Cells. Words can't explain the emotional state I began to endure as he now needed my emotional support to handle cancer and the recent reentry of his father into his life after being absent for twenty-three years. I didn't connect and continued to work harder at the business.

Three months later my first grandchild was born and my daughter suffered with depression. I continued to work even harder. Three months later my granddaughters father had a mental breakdown and murdered a close family member. This heightened my daughter's emotional need and once again I continued to work harder at the business. Working hard at the office kept my mind occupied from all my personal attacks but was I really being productive?

    I was showing up every day, making decisions, carrying the load of the staff members and students, but nothing was improving. I gained fifty pounds, began to fight major health issues and became functionally depressed. I found myself losing motivation and passion for what I was doing and was just simply moving through the world unbalanced. How could a top National Board-Certified Teacher with experience of working on a turnaround team for low performing schools now be a founder of a low performing school? Easy; by losing hope, direction and fighting alone.

Year three should have made me loss my mind. During that time, I should have thrown in the towel, but only by grace was I able to make it through. I believe we are constantly a work in progress and even now I am still dealing with me; however, I can say once I became better and balanced, everything around me started to get better. Not only did things improve and become better, everything attached to me began to win. If this chapter motivates any current or future bosses, let the inspiration be to take care of you first as you can't lead from your broken spaces. Fix you and the rest will follow.

Chapter 9: 21 Leadership Lessons Learned

1. Never pay the contractor until the job is done.

My first building renovation brought on excitement and joy. I was so excited to open a school and only thought about the end results. Not having prior experience with renovations or contractors, I trusted the individual hired to do right by me. I entered a contract with an individual who did not have enough personal resources to carry the job and needed me to make payments up front. During the job, items previously discussed were changed to benefit the contractor and not the school. Work was left incomplete and in the end, we had to call someone else in the complete the job in order to receive our certificate of occupancy. I could not hold the contractor accountable as he had already received 90% of his expenses. Hiring another person to finish the job ended up costing me more money than budgeted. Never pay the contractor until the job is done.

2. **Be clear about everything; never assume everyone wants what you want.**

Creating mission statements, vision statements, policies and procedures is the start of every organizational operation process. As a leader you are always sharing thoughts on what the vision will look like. You provide employee handbooks outlining employee expectations. It's easy to assume everyone understands what is being presented and expected. It's easy to assume if an employee sought out your place of business to work then they wanted to be part of implementing the vision. Unfortunately, that is not always the case. Many just want a job with a dependable check. Don't assume anything and clearly state what you want. Just be sure if you expect it then be prepared to inspect it.

3. **Doing the right thing is hard but necessary. - Make the tough decisions.**

As a boss you will make hundreds of decisions daily. While some of these decisions will be simple, requiring little thought and effort; some will be hard, emotional and difficult. As a boss, your bottom line responsibility is to make decisions that will keep the organization moving forward. You must lead with your head while staying in touch with your emotions. As a school leader, I learned our sole purpose is to improve the lives of the children we serve. All decisions must be made with that in mind. If it's not improving students then let it go. I had to terminate several people that were very close to me but were not being productive for the business. It was extremely hard to do but necessary for organizational growth. Once the tough decision was made and the people were removed; the earth sent what was needed.

4. **Listen to your gut always.**

   Your gut is your internal guide decision making. All of your life lessons, experiences, and knowledge have been collected inside of your unconscious mind. Your gut is the experiences collected together providing instinct. Learn to tap into your gut when making decisions. Mediate, reflect and always follow your gut.

5. **Understand the competition will steal your ideas.**

   When doing great things, the competition will always be on the prowl to steal your ideas and make them their own. Don't let this stop your shine. In other words, don't spend time worrying and complaining. Oprah didn't spend time worrying about Ellen or other talk show hosts. She was a trailblazer who opened paths for others to follow. Keep growing, keep moving and keep progressing.

6. **Be selfish.**

Find a healthy balance and always look out for self-first. No one will take care of you better than you will take care of yourself. Time is valuable like money; so protect your time always. I learned I am a magnet for broken people. Everyone in my life, both personal and professional, depend on me to plug into them and make them better. This can be exhausting. Prior to learning my purpose, I allowed others to drain me. I had a hard time saying, "No, not now." I would sacrifice my wants, needs and desires in order to fulfill someone else's. At the end of the day, the people I gave the greatest sacrifice repaid me with pain and disappointment. Now I've learned it is imperative I take care of me first. You simply cannot give what you do not have.

7. **Learn to be good at spotting talent.**

Make it a point to surround yourself with the very best. Build a team that is willing to grind with you and make the business shine. There are many talents people bring to the table and it is important to learn how to identify their strengths. Once it's identified, you may then nurture those strengths to improve the organization. As a leader of an arts school I was always amazed to find artistic abilities in my non-teaching staff. My data manager is an excellent artist and often highlights her work in our art shows. Become good at spotting talent and knowing how to use it.

8. **Make sure the right people are standing at the canvas holding the right brush.**

In an arts school this is equivalent to making sure the right people are on the bus and in the right seat. As a leader of an arts school our students are like canvases. Teachers are creating master pieces as they paint, draw, or mold students into healthy productive human beings. It is imperative to pair the right teacher with the right student canvas and ensure they are using the right brush technique to get the greatest gain.

9. **Rid the site of toxic behavior/people.**

   Toxic behaviors/people will kill any organization. Toxic people create toxic environments. When toxic people intermingle with healthy people the whole system suffers. A leader's number one responsibility in a toxic environment is to kill the building cancer and build a healthy culture. So, what is the chemotherapy needed for building cancer?

   - Check into every aspect of the program.
   - Stay connected. Allow people to do their job but always be aware of what is going on

in the field. Use all your senses, what you see, what you hear, what you feel to heighten your emotional and business awareness.

- Once you identify a toxic person get rid of them immediately.
- Let go of the wrong people to make room for the right people.

10. Boss doesn't mean healer.

As a school leader it's not your job to change people. Hold staff accountable for their own personal and professional growth. If they are not willing or are incapable of growing; help them find a different career. Just remember, everyone is responsible for fixing themselves.

Building a school village of healthy tribe members creates a culture that is conducive to high levels of teaching and learning.

11. Quick to fire and slow to hire.

In year five I completed an organizational purge. In seven months I terminated nine of twelve people. This practice was the first year I had done such a task. In the past, I would identify toxic staff but would hold on to them until the end of the year out of fear. The fear of not being able to find a replacement. I did that for four years and never met my goals. That practice created a lot of stress. The year I decided to terminate anyone who showed signs of not being capable of change was the year my goals were finally achieved. Sometimes when I had to terminate staff and bring in a replacement, I would teach the class for a few months as they job shadowed, to ensure I found the perfect replacement. The replacement staff was also able to work as a long-term sub for sixty days. This allowed me time to see if they were capable of handling our student population and if they were healthy individuals. If all went well at the end of the sixty days a full contract would be offered.

12. **Maintain high emotional intelligence and strong interpersonal skills.**

Self-management is a pillar of emotional intelligence and interpersonal skills. Self-management is the ability to control your emotions when the situation is not aligned to what behaviors would be considered acceptable for a given situation. Are you able to you control your anger, or hid your frustration?

Social awareness is the ability to build rapport in relationships and manage those relationships. Emotions have the ability to be transferred from person to person. Everyone must take responsibility for interacting with others and building a positive work environment. Finally, have self-awareness.

In self-awareness, the key is to know yourself and become keenly aware of your own mental state. You can't give what you don't have.

13. Hold everyone accountable for carrying their own weight.

Everyone has a job to do and if everyone does it; it'll keep the organization moving forward. If one person stops doing his/her job it creates a breakdown within the organization. This breakdown causes other teammates to pick up someone else's burden. Carrying someone else's weight causes loss in motivation and animosity towards coworkers.

In order to ensure teachers carried their own weight I did not allow them to send their challenging students to each other. This activity was banned and instead we have a very integral discipline plan in place. The discipline plan lists tier one, two and three offenses with the appropriate steps to take. If teachers use their classroom management procedures, communicate with parents, consistently enforce the school rules and follow the discipline plan, student behaviors would be minimal. If a teacher sends their difficult students to a coworker, they give their power to the coworker. This causes students not to respect or trust the teacher. The teacher following the discipline expectations now has her problems and a coworker's problem and that's just not fair.

14. Expect the bad and be prepared.

Learn early how to play chess. When making one move always think about the impact of that move and be prepared for your next one. I am a very optimist person who's always looking for the good or positive side. This has often caused me great deal of pain when blindsided by a negative response or action. I had to learn to go into every situation expecting the bad. That expectation made me analysis worst case scenarios and how to handle them. In many cases I didn't have to operate from the worst but I was prepared to do so.

15. Be comfortable with confrontation.

This was one of my greatest lessons. Being an anti-social person, I find comfort in being alone and not having to deal with other peoples' emotions and feelings. I am not an emotional person, therefore, I do not like confrontation at all. What I didn't realize was since this was my personality; I gave off energy telling others of my deposition. I believe this made people be disrespectful at times as they knew I didn't like dealing with confrontation. Staff members did some of the craziest things and I wouldn't deal with it. Once I embraced my dislike and determined enough was enough, I came in everyday ready for war. Initially teachers thought

"Stacey's tripping today" or "Stacey is on one today". Disrespect and non-productivity were no longer going to be tolerated. It didn't take me long to notice as soon as I confronted the issues contributing to unproductive behaviors, things improved for the better.

16. It's always about the kids.

The business of school is about children. Changing the lives of children and giving hope to children. The students are the schools VIS (very important student). Without the students the school would not exist. This is especially true for a charter school. As a school of choice, charters give parents additional options for finding a school that meets the needs of their children. Parents make the choice to join the charter school's family and that choice should not be taken lightly.

During the fifth year, I experienced an issue where several staff members personal problems overshadowed their ability to provide for the needs of our students. A vast amount of time was spent trying to help the teacher adjust. Before long it became about the conveniences for the adult than the student. Operating from that perspective never wins. Keep the kids the main thing always.

17. Believe at all times and remain focused.

There will be times when your best plans simply do not work. You may begin to think things are just not going how they should and if not checked, this will open the door of doubt. Negative thoughts will begin to slip into your mind as you question yourself about your ability to lead. During these times look in the mirror and say, "Knock it off (insert your name here). I believe in myself. I believe in the vision and I know that it will work out." Refocus yourself and keep moving.

18. **It's okay to fail but it's not okay to quit.**

Some of your best lessons will come in those moments of failure. If you allow yourself to reflect and grow, failure will propel you to the next level. In fact, if you want to be great, figure out a way to fail faster or more often. It is okay to fail but you cannot quit. Quitting is not an option!

19. Always walk and talk like a boss.

As the leader everyone is always watching your every move. They are always listening to everything you say. Your actions must exude confidence. Your sound must reveal professionalism and you must always walk in authority.

20. Know when to seek help.

It's lonely at the top. When things are heavy it's always good to have a voice of reason. Someone who will tell you the truth even when you don't want to hear it. If you bring in outside advisors be sure to listen to them. When you are burdened down and have lost your view from the balcony a different set of eyes and ears might be the solution needed to get back on track. One of my advisors gave me the hard truth regularly. He challenged me to make decisions I knew I had to make but was avoiding as a way to steer from confrontation. Once I made the decision to follow the advice, changes occurred quickly and for the better. As a charter school the leader often plays the role of principal and superintendent. Not having the district office as an infrastructure to provide additional support can be challenging. Be open to seeking outside help if needed. I needed help with curriculum mapping and in the process found a nationally known author on curriculum mapping. This person had done all the research on the topic and was known for helping universities and other entities. I took a chance and called to see if they provided support to small schools, and before I knew it a deal was made. Dare to take risks and dare to be different. Do whatever you must to save the children.

21. Do real evaluations and not fluff.

Teachers are responsible for getting better and they depend on leaders to be honest and straightforward in their feedback.

Chapter 10: The Charge

Opening a Charter School from ground zero has been one of the most challenging endeavors I have had. It has also been the most rewarding and an honor to do. To date we have made a lot of growth, although not quite where we want to be. There is no doubt this task was given to me as a vision from God Himself, and I have enjoyed walking in my purpose. It hasn't been easy and I know there is still much more to learn. For those who are contemplating following a dream or opening a school, I encourage you to learn the business side of the endeavor and be the best entrepreneur you can be.

www.ingramcontent.com/pod-product-compliance
Lightning Source LLC
Chambersburg PA
CBHW021019090426
42738CB00007B/835